P9-CQY-498

# CONTENTS

# WELCOME TO FALL GUYS!

In *Fall Guys* you enter a series of colorful and chaotic minigames. Competing online against others, some players are eliminated each round until a winner is found!

It's very easy to pick up, but it's not enough just to be able to complete each round—you have to do it better than the rest. And you'll be up against players who know every step of those minigames!

Any tips you pick up can give you the edge—so with the help of this book, you can become Master of the Beans!

GET INTO THE COLORFUL CHAOS!

VICTORY CAN BE YOURS!

Fall Guys was developed by the London-based company Mediatonic. It combines elements from game shows like *Takeshi's Castle* and *Wipeout*, playground games like tag and red rover, and computer games like *Mario Party* to create an online multiplayer experience like no other!

GETTING HOOKED ON THIS GAME IS A SLIPPERY SLOPE ...

WEIRD NEW WORLDS ARE ADDED ALL THE TIME!

Every few months a new season launches, with new rounds and a new theme. Since the original wave, they've added Medieval, Winter, Future, Jungle, and Party—but the old rounds are kept in, so the game just keeps expanding.

There have also been several crossovers, allowing you to obtain costumes for your avatar based on *Sonic*, *Among Us*, *Cuphead*, *Godzilla*, *LittleBigPlanet*, and more.

FEEL LIKE A MUG?

# YOUR BEAN

You play as a cute little bean. But with up to 60 beans playing at the same time, it's helpful to stand out from the crowd.

faceplate

hands for grabbing

round body for rolling

short legs for tumbling

Crown Kudos

At the start you can choose your bean's colors and pattern. You can change them at any time, and you can earn new ones as you go. Some are rewards for progress; some can be bought with the in-game currency—Crowns and Kudos.

You can also collect costumes. If you think they look ridiculously impractical for tackling an obstacle course—you're absolutely right! The creators of *Fall Guys* were inspired by an old British game show called *It's a Knockout* where the contestants had to race in oversized foam costumes.

# HOW TO PLAY

**You can choose to play solo or as a four-person squad. There are also duo and trio challenges as well as limited-time special shows.**

The gameplay is simple—there are just four basic actions. The main two are **run** and **jump**.

YOU JUST GOTTA MOVE ...

The **grab** function comes into play in a lot of rounds. You can use this to grab onto certain movable objects, catch a ride on a swinging trapeze, hang from an edge and climb up, snatch something from another player, or even hold onto another player to stop them moving!

TINY HANDS CAN GRAB BIG THINGS!

The **dive** function can be very handy—you can use it to dodge obstacles, extend your jumps, or even leap over the finish line!

THROW YOURSELF AROUND!

When you start a tournament, a round will be randomly selected. Which will depend on how many players are involved—every tournament starts with 40–60 players, so a Race will usually come first because those are the ones that involve the largest numbers.

FALLING INTO A NEW TOURNAMENT...

GET OFF TO A GOOD START!

**24 QUALIFIED**

ARE YOU OUT? OR STILL IN?

After every round, a certain number of players will be eliminated. How many varies depending on the round. Sometimes the first 70% of players to finish will go through and the rest will be knocked out. Sometimes all the ones who survive the round will go through. Sometimes you'll be pitted against one other player and have to knock them out.

And then another randomly-selected round begins!

The rounds fall into different categories:

## RACE △ △ △ △ △

Get past different obstacles and make it to the finish line. Falling sets you back to the last checkpoint.

## SURVIVAL △ △ △ △ △

Stay in a dangerous environment. Falling eliminates you! The ones who survive to the end go through.

## HUNT △ △ △ △ △

Carry out a specified task, such as bursting bubbles or hitting buttons. Qualification is usually points-based.

## LOGIC △ △ △ △ △

Memory games where you must find a safe place to stand based on the information you're given. All survivors qualify.

## TEAM △ △ △ △ △

Players are randomly put into two, three, or four teams and play against each other. The winning team goes through; some or all of the others may be eliminated.

## FINAL △ △ △ △ △

These rounds may take any of the above forms—but at the end, there will be a winner!

# TUNDRA RUN

## GETTING THROUGH THIS ICE-THEMED RACE IS SNOW BIG DEAL WITH OUR TIPS!

This race has several different types of obstacles, but none of them are too challenging. Take the easiest route and you've got a good chance of qualifying: the players who fail are often the ones who are impatient and try to take it too quickly.

**MIDDLE ROUTE OR SIDE ROUTE?**

## GAME TIPS

**1** Don't worry too much about the snowballs (replaced by fruit in some variants)—you shouldn't have problems dodging those. Focus on avoiding other players, who can easily get in your way when rushing through the narrow passages.

## 👑 STAT ATTACK

**NUMBER OF PLAYERS:** 40-60
**HOW MANY QUALIFY:** 70%
**MAX LENGTH OF ROUND:** 3:00
**INTRODUCED:** SEASON 3
**DIFFICULTY RATING:** 1/5

**2** The section with the punching gloves has much easier, but slower, paths around the sides. If you try the middle route, be aware of which gloves have most recently punched, because those ones are less likely to punch again while you're on them.

**3** The slope with the moving fan at the top has a block on either side. Run over to one of these blocks and get on the other side of it—this will stop you sliding down when the fan passes. As soon as the fan has moved away, run up the slope!

**4** Make a running jump onto the big moving fan—if you try to do it with a standing jump, you're unlikely to get far enough. This makes it more difficult to time your jump, so get to know the movement patterns of the fan and the obstacles.

DON'T GET BLOWN OFF COURSE.

IS IT COLD IN HERE?

**! TOP TIP**

DIVING WHILE IN THE AIR CAN HELP YOU REACH THE FINISH LINE HERE.

# DIZZY HEIGHTS

## THIS COURSE OF ROTATING DISCS WILL MAKE YOUR HEAD SPIN!

The main sections of this course are made up of spinning discs. The most important thing is to always run in the direction the disc is spinning. Even going a short distance takes ages when running against the spin, and it's always quicker to let the disc take you back round.

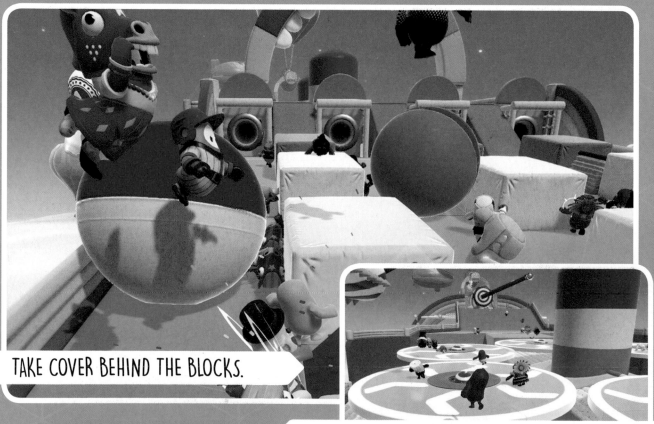

TAKE COVER BEHIND THE BLOCKS.

GO WITH THE ARROWS, NOT AGAINST THEM!

# GAME TIPS

**1** You can simply run from one disc to the next in the first area. But it's easy to mistime this and get carried back around, so jumping is safer. The second set of discs have gaps between them and have to be jumped.

**2** In between those two sets of discs you will find a slope where cannons fire colored balls at you. It's better to stick to the middle two channels—they have two side areas you can duck into for protection, whereas the channels at the edges only have one.

HOP OVER THE ROTATING BEAMS.

## TOP TIP

THERE'S A HIDDEN GAP BEFORE THE FINAL SET OF DISCS—DON'T FALL DOWN IT!

**3** If you've played a course before, you may think the intro isn't worth watching. Wrong! You can use it to check for variants, since additional obstacles may be placed in the course—in this case, you may find rotating beams or pendulums.

**4** During the intro, you should look out for which way the final disc in the second set of discs is turning. If it's going clockwise, take the left path through the discs. But if it's counter-clockwise, take the right path.

## ♛ STAT ATTACK

**NUMBER OF PLAYERS:** 40–60
**HOW MANY QUALIFY:** 70%
**MAX LENGTH OF ROUND:** 3:00
**INTRODUCED:** Beta version
**DIFFICULTY RATING:** 2/5

# FREEZY PEAK

## YOU'LL NEED TO BE IN PEAK CONDITION TO GET THROUGH THIS RACE!

This Arctic-themed race has several different paths through it, and the first one will depend on your spawn point. Some of the paths feature horizontal boxing gloves, while others have vertical ones that punch up from the ground. The final section is a race to the top of a tower.

## GAME TIPS

**1** When walking through the horizontal boxing gloves, keep to the middle (this can be tricky if lots of players are around) and watch the pattern of the gloves as they punch. The vertical ones also have a pattern.

GREAT SUPPORT FROM THE FANS!

**2** The next section also has multiple routes. Some force you to run up a backward conveyor belt while a cannon fires at you—these are slow but straightforward. The others have fans that blow you onto Slingus Flinguses, which can be trickier.

**3** The second of the two fans that carry you up to the spiral chute can be hard to hit correctly, so it can pay to stop before it. Just make sure you get the right angle and there are no snowballs coming!

**4** On the chute you can choose to either walk on the left and dodge snowballs, or on the right and dodge boxing gloves. The gloves are easier—wait for each one to punch and go back in, then you'll have just enough time to get past before they punch again.

I'VE GOT A MOUNTAIN TO CLIMB! LITERALLY.

## ! TOP TIP

DIVE TO REACH THE FINAL PLATFORM—YOUR GUY WILL RECOVER FASTER.

NOT FEELING THE GLOVE ...

# FRUIT CHUTE

## YOU MUST BE A REAL 'NANA IF YOU DON'T LOVE THIS PEACH OF A GAME!

The aim of this game is to reach the finish while avoiding fruit being fired from cannons! Sounds simple? Try running up a slope with a melon hurtling your way! You'll face way more than your apple-a-day in this round ...

FIND A ROUTE THROUGH THE CHUTE.

## GAME TIPS

**1** When the game begins, get a head start by launching onto the conveyor belt with a jump-dive. After that, move to one side of the course—either one will work just fine. Logs roll down the center of the conveyor belt—and that's where most of the fruit goes, too!

##  STAT ATTACK

**NUMBER OF PLAYERS:** 12–30
**HOW MANY QUALIFY:** 60%
**MAX LENGTH OF ROUND:** 3:00
**INTRODUCED:** SEASON 1
**DIFFICULTY RATING:** 2/5

**2** The cannons fire out watermelons, peaches, and bananas. Avoid them all, even if it means running sideways. It's fairly easy to guess where the peaches will roll, but it's tricky trying to predict the movement of the other fruit, which bounces around all over the place.

**3** The pink pyramids at the sides are your friends! You can briefly pause behind them for protection if you spot some fruit coming your way. And if you're standing in front of one and are on the end of a "fruit punch," the pyramids can work as a safety net to stop you falling off.

**4** Toward the end of the round, the cannons fire out a single volley of strawberries and blueberries. Don't panic because they move in a straight line, so once you've spotted them, it's not difficult to stay out of their way.

**EVERYTHING'S GONE BANANAS!**

I'M BREAKING OUT SOME SWEET MOVES!

**TOP TIP**

IT'S USUALLY BETTER TO RUN AWAY FROM THE FRUIT INSTEAD OF TRYING TO JUMP OVER IT.

# PARTY PROMENADE

## LET'S GET THIS PARTY STARTED ... AND FINISHED AS QUICKLY AS POSSIBLE!

This party-themed race is one of the simplest starter rounds—none of the obstacles is especially frustrating. However, there are some choices to be made along the way that can give you the edge—and getting to those see-saws first is a real advantage!

PRETTY FLY FOR A FALL GUY!

# GAME TIPS

**GET IN THE SWING OF IT!**

**1** After you're thrown into the air and land in a bowl, there's a green pipe at the bottom. This one is the easiest to reach and it will take you to a slimy slope. But the yellow pipes will take you straight to the see-saws.

**2** Later, there's a section where you can either use the Big Swingus to cross, or go around the sides with the flipper gates. The gates alternate between spinning clockwise and counter-clockwise, so watch out and don't get knocked off.

**GOTTA FIND THE RIGHT BALANCE.**

**3** If you decide to swing, go right to one end of the Swingus and grab on. Don't jump off at the other side—just release and let yourself drop. This will place you near one of the ramps for the next section.

**4** The toughest part is the swing from the top of the ramp to the yellow funnel. If you make this jump, the pipe will take you almost to the finish line. If you miss it, take the see-saws over to the yellow ramp and carefully climb onto the pipe instead.

## ! TOP TIP

AT SOME POINTS YOU HAVE TO TURN AND GO THE OTHER WAY—FOLLOW THE ARROWS.

## ♔ STAT ATTACK

**NUMBER OF PLAYERS:** 40–60
**HOW MANY QUALIFY:** 70%
**MAX LENGTH OF ROUND:** 5:00
**INTRODUCED:** SEASON 6
**DIFFICULTY RATING:** 1/5

# LILY LEAPERS

## MAKE LIKE A FROG AND HOP FROM LILY PAD TO LILY PAD TO WIN THIS RACE!

This race is all based on a single technique—bouncing off lily pads. Some of the sections aren't easy, so take your time because a lot of players struggle with this one. You can always bounce once and land back on the same lily pad to get your bearings before attempting to bounce to the next one.

## GAME TIPS

**1** You can dive while bouncing. This combo is essential to mastering Lily Leapers—several jumps are difficult or impossible without it. The best moment to hit "dive" is just before you reach the peak of your bounce.

 WATCH THE ONES THAT MOVE.

**2** The middle route through the initial area is the most straightforward one, but there are side routes which are quicker but harder. If you fall on those sections, you'll be sent to the middle route. New players should probably focus on the middle.

## ★ STAT ATTACK

**NUMBER OF PLAYERS:** 40–60
**HOW MANY QUALIFY:** 70%
**MAX LENGTH OF ROUND:** 5:00
**INTRODUCED:** SEASON 5
**DIFFICULTY RATING:** 4/5

**3** After that opening section, things start to get challenging. There are lily pads on the ground that move and you must bounce on them in order to get to the ones that are moving in the air. Wait for them to move close to each other before jumping.

**4** The final section has angled lily pads that need to be hit perfectly to send you onto the next one. The side routes here are slower but easier—so unless you're a lily pad ninja, they're definitely the best option.

**TOP TIP**

BOUNCING ON THE EDGE OF A LILY PAD, RATHER THAN THE MIDDLE, LAUNCHES YOU AWAY FROM IT.

FULL THROTTLE TOWARD THE FINISH LINE!

IF YOU FALL DOWN, YOU CAN BOUNCE BACK.

# KNIGHT FEVER

## YOU CAN BE KING OF THE CASTLE IN THIS MEDIEVAL-THEMED RACE!

Knight Fever is full of sharp pointy things, but the main obstacles to watch out for are the drawbridges just before the finish line—they seem simple enough, but timing is everything! This race has lots of potential variants, including extra axes, see-saws, blizzard fans, and Big Yeetuses.

WHO'S FOR THE CHOP?

## GAME TIPS

**1** On the first section with the swinging axes, you need to be either at the front or way behind if you want to run down the side—doing that gives you more time between passes. However, if the run is crowded, you risk other players knocking into you and pushing you over the edge.

**2** The logs with rotating spikes are also difficult when crowded. The best thing to do is to stop and wait when a spike is in your path, but be careful someone doesn't push you into them from behind. And don't try to jump them!

**3** When approaching the two Thicc Bonkuses, go to one side of the path and wait until the first Bonkus has just swung away from it. Run at this point and you should be able to clear this whole section.

**4** The drawbridges at the end don't stay closed for long, and you want it to be closing just as you reach the middle. So head for one that's raised and leap on it the moment it's low enough to run along.

A BRIDGE TOO FAR FOR SOME PLAYERS!

THIS ROUND IS A KNIGHTMARE!

**TOP TIP**

WATCH OUT FOR VARIANT DRAWBRIDGES—SOME DON'T FULLY CLOSE AND SOME DON'T MOVE IN SYNC.

△ △ △ △ △ △

# HIT PARADE

## THIS CLASSIC OBSTACLE RACE IS A BIG HIT WITH US!

One of the earliest and easiest races, Hit Parade is also one of the shortest—none of its sections is especially long or complicated. If you work out your strategy and stick to it, this one shouldn't pose you too many problems.

WATCH OUT FOR VARIANTS OF THIS ROUND.

GET INTO THE SWING OF THINGS!

**1** First of all, don't worry about the beams you have to run across and hop between. If you drop down and run up the slope, you'll lose little or no time and you won't have to contend with hordes of other players on the narrow beams.

**2** Before you reach the revolving doors, pick a side and go that way—the center is slower in this case. And watch the movement of the sliding wall at the end. If you get there too late and the wall blocks your path, just wait for it to open again.

DIVING CAN HELP ON THE FINAL SLOPE.

**!**

## TOP TIP
IF YOU GET THE SPINNING DISCS, DON'T TRY TO USE THEM FOR EXTRA SPEED— HOP OVER THEM IF YOU CAN.

**3** Take it steady on the section with the pendulums. They're not hard to avoid if you watch them and stop when necessary. Getting through this section without being knocked into the gutter will usually be enough to qualify.

**4** There are lots of variants for this race, so it's another one where it pays to watch the opening cutscene to see if anything's different. You may find pendulums in the first section, for instance, or spinning discs instead of the revolving doors.

## ♛ STAT ATTACK

**NUMBER OF PLAYERS:** 40-60
**HOW MANY QUALIFY:** 70%
**MAX LENGTH OF ROUND:** 3:00
**INTRODUCED:** Beta version
**DIFFICULTY RATING:** 1/5

# FULL TILT

## DON'T LET YOUR MOOD DIP IF YOU CAN'T WIN THIS ONE—USE OUR TIPS!

This is one of the most frustrating rounds in *Fall Guys*!
It's mostly made up of 360-degree see-saws that can tilt
in any direction. A lot of players fall a *lot* of times on
this round, so don't worry too much if everyone gets
a head start on you. You can catch up!

## GAME TIPS

DON'T GET DINGED OFF THE DISC!

**1** How well you do on Full Tilt depends on where you spawn. The players on the front row will all leap on first. If you're not at the front, by the time you reach the see-saw it'll be tilting so much you're unlikely to make it.

### ♕ STAT ATTACK

**NUMBER OF PLAYERS:** 40-60
**HOW MANY QUALIFY:** 70%
**MAX LENGTH OF ROUND:** 3:00
**INTRODUCED:** SEASON 6
**DIFFICULTY RATING:** 3/5

**2** Some see-saws have donut bumpers and rotating beams. You can dodge them—or if they're going in the right direction, you can get in front of them and let them push you from behind. If you time this right, you can get them to throw you to the next platform.

**3** The see-saws with the force fields on them often tilt in a way that makes your jump impossible. If this does happen, you'll just have to level out the see-saw or jump across to the other one. Remember you can go around the force fields!

**4** Several see-saws can be avoided entirely by using the drums underneath. In some situations you can only use these ones by jumping and then diving to get a little extra distance—but this is a good technique to learn anyway.

THESE DISCS CARRY A LOT OF RISKS!

**! TOP TIP**

THE CENTER PATH IS THE FASTEST IF YOU SPAWN IN THE FRONT ROW. BUT THE SIDE PATHS ARE SAFER.

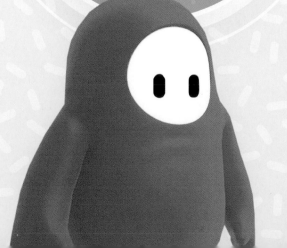

GO FOR THE LESS BUSY ROUTE.

# WALL GUYS

## THIS GAME WILL DRIVE YOU UP THE WALL—LITERALLY!

In this race you have to get over a series of walls by shoving blocks against them and then climbing over. But if you push a block into place, others can use it too, so you'll be helping your opponents. This is a rare example of a round where it's better *not* to be in the front row at the start!

YOU MAY HAVE TO FIGHT FOR SPACE!

# GAME TIPS

**1** Progress is quicker if you let others push the blocks for you—but this depends on them actually doing it! Newer players who have yet to master this race may do it, or someone may just decide to be nice and helpful.

**2** Of course, this will lead to a situation where the first players over the wall are the ones who've let others move the blocks for them—so they'll have to wait for someone else to do it or do it themselves the next time!

**3** The grab-and-climb-up function is essential here. The taller blocks can be climbed this way, meaning you don't need to use the smaller ones as steps. Often a wall can be climbed by jumping and grabbing onto the edge, too.

DON'T HANG AROUND—GET OVER THE WALL.

WOW, THAT BLEW UP!

**4** With most players all focusing on the same route, it can get hectic and you can get jostled off—so you may prefer to go off to one side and build your own path. The others probably won't even notice.

## ! TOP TIP

NOTE THAT THE WALLS GRADUALLY SINK INTO THE GROUND, MEANING THEY GET EASIER TO CLIMB.

## ♛ STAT ATTACK

**NUMBER OF PLAYERS:** 15–30
**HOW MANY QUALIFY:** 60%
**MAX LENGTH OF ROUND:** 5:00
**INTRODUCED:** SEASON 2
**DIFFICULTY RATING:** 3/5

# SHORT CIRCUIT

## A RACE SO SHORT, YOU HAVE TO DO IT TWICE!

Short Circuit is like a lot of obstacle races in *Fall Guys,* except it goes round in a loop and you get to do it all again. The players who succeed here learn from what they got wrong on the first lap and fix it for the second!

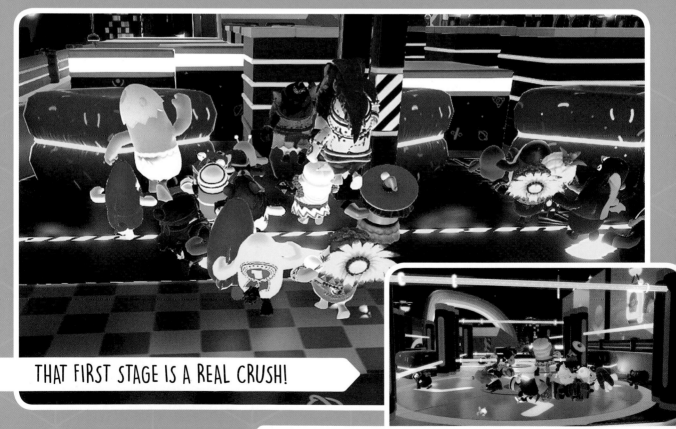

THAT FIRST STAGE IS A REAL CRUSH!

REMEMBER, RUN WITH THE DISC, NOT AGAINST IT.

## GAME TIPS

**1** The most annoying part tends to be the maze of blocks at the start, because they move and gaps can close in front of you. You can try climbing up and over, though others trying the same thing may get in your way.

**2** Three of the four corners contain punching gloves which can hit you backward or forward—it's safest to avoid them completely by going to the right of the conveyor belt and cutting the corner with a well-timed jump at the end.

DON'T STOP—GO FOR THE FINISH!

**TOP TIP**

WATCH OUT FOR THE FORWARD-FACING SLINGUS FLINGUSES AT THE END AND JUMP ON THEM.

**3** The light beams are very tricky to avoid, especially on the second gate which has double beams. The best approach is to jump and dive between them, but the timing is made much harder by the spinning discs, so there's a lot of luck involved!

**4** The buttons between the two sets of gravity zones will switch between pink (high gravity) and blue (low gravity). If you've just been through a blue zone, sabotage players behind you by switching it to pink. In a pink zone you'll have to wait for the gate to open.

## STAT ATTACK

**NUMBER OF PLAYERS:** 30-45
**HOW MANY QUALIFY:** 60%
**MAX LENGTH OF ROUND:** 5:00
**INTRODUCED:** SEASON 4
**DIFFICULTY RATING:** 2/5

# HOVERBOARD HEROES

## IT'S IMPOSSIBLE TO GET "BOARD" PLAYING THIS GAME!

In this round, all you have to do is stay on the giant hoverboard as it moves very slowly across a lake of slime. The challenge is to not get swept off by any of the obstacles the hoverboard passes on the way!

## GAME TIPS

**1** The first round of obstacles is the light bars, which aren't too bad. If you're near the front of the board, you can afford a couple of misses. Just watch out for the double set because you will have to jump between them.

ANOTHER BOARD MEETING ...

**2** Next there's an island you must climb over. It's best to approach on the right since there are two conveyor belts and the first one will send you left. Make sure you don't go too fast and hit the slime slide before the board arrives!

## ♕ STAT ATTACK

**NUMBER OF PLAYERS:** 20–30
**HOW MANY QUALIFY:**
ALL SURVIVORS
**MAX LENGTH OF ROUND:** 2:20
**INTRODUCED:** SEASON 4
**DIFFICULTY RATING:** 2/5

**3** Almost immediately there's another island with a low-gravity zone. And right after that you face swinging light bars, which may swing vertically or horizontally. Stand in the middle to avoid the vertical ones, or at the edge for horizontal ones (but watch out for others nudging you off).

**4** There's a hidden gap on the final island, and you need the flippers to launch you across it. Don't try to jump it or you'll be eliminated right at the end! Simply stand by a flipper and wait for it to activate.

**! TOP TIP**

AVOID THE CANNON FIRE BY TURNING THE CAMERA SO YOU CAN SEE MISSILES COMING.

YOU'RE ON SOUND FOOTING THERE ...

YOU DON'T HAVE TO BE FIRST—JUST SURVIVE!

# BIG SHOTS

## YOU'LL NEED COURAGE UNDER FIRE TO GET THROUGH THIS ONE!

Big Shots is one of the simplest rounds! You spawn on a see-saw and cannons fire planets, stars, giant game controllers, and other stuff at you. All you have to do is avoid getting knocked into the slime. If the round times out before 40% of players are eliminated, all survivors qualify.

SEE? IT'S A SEE-SAW.

## GAME TIPS

**1** Tactically, this is one of the easiest rounds to tackle. Don't stand at the rear of the see-saw, because that'll make it easier for the projectiles to knock you off. And don't stand too close to the front, because other players might knock you in.

**2** The ends of the see-saw can dip into the slime, so avoid those. If one side of the see-saw raises, head over to the other side, but not too far. The middle of the board is best here.

## ★ STAT ATTACK

**NUMBER OF PLAYERS:** 14–30
**HOW MANY QUALIFY:** 60%
**MAX LENGTH OF ROUND:** 1:30
**INTRODUCED:** SEASON 4
**DIFFICULTY RATING:** 2/5

**3** One variant adds a swinging ax right in the center of the see-saw. This does make the middle more dangerous—but don't change your tactics too much. Stand clear enough to make sure you don't get pushed into the ax, but otherwise stay around the middle.

**4** Another variant has two cannons that fire with less power. However, this is a bad thing because the projectiles tend to land on the see-saw, and can drag you to the edges if you don't get away from them.

MOVE TO THE HIGHER END.

I'LL GIVE IT MY BEST SHOT!

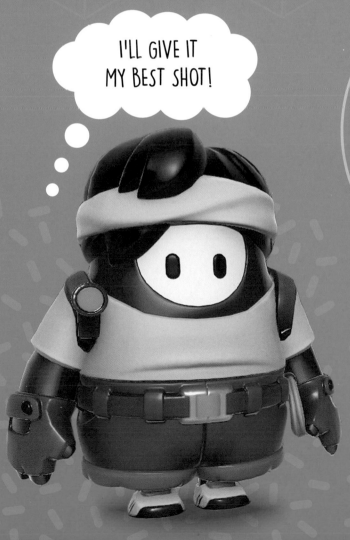

**TOP TIP**

THERE'S A SLIGHTLY EASIER VARIANT OF THIS ROUND WHERE THE CANNONS FIRE FRUIT.

# ROLL OUT

## LET THE GOOD TIMES ROLL, BUT DON'T GET ROLLED OFF!

In this round, players spawn on a roller in five sections. Three of the sections turn in one direction, and two turn in the opposite direction. If you stay on one section for too long, a wall or a gap will force you off. Stay on the roller to win!

STAND WHERE YOU CAN SEE THE GAPS.

NO ROCK, JUST ROLL.

## GAME TIPS

**1** Make sure your camera is positioned so you can see what's coming up on your own roller and the nearest one. If you can't see the gaps coming, you'll fall into them! A slightly sideways and downward view is helpful.

**2** It's best to pick two rollers and hop between them—hanging around the border between two rollers makes it easier to move quickly. And stay away from the middle roller—it's often the busiest, with people pushing each other off.

IF YOU END UP HERE—MOVE!

**TOP TIP**

THERE'S ALSO A RACE VERSION OF THIS ROUND (ROLL ON) AND A FINAL (ROLL OFF).

**3** By sticking to two rollers you can learn what obstacles are on them, and use the same techniques to avoid falling until you qualify. Be careful if you get the variant where giant fruit are fired at the roller.

**4** Because of the rollers' movement, jumps can be hard to judge, so don't take risks. This is good advice on any Survival round—you don't need the edge on other players, you just have to not fall.

## ♛ STAT ATTACK

**NUMBER OF PLAYERS:** 30–50
**HOW MANY QUALIFY:** 60%
**MAX LENGTH OF ROUND:** 2:30
**INTRODUCED:** Beta version
**DIFFICULTY RATING:** 4/5

# STOMPIN' GROUND

## NO IFS OR BUTS—YOU'VE GOT TO AVOID GETTING HEAD-BUTTED OUT!

In this Survival round, players spawn in a circular arena with three rhinos in pens. When the rhinos are released, they'll randomly charge at the players who must avoid being knocked out of the arena. All players who manage this, qualify for the next round.

## GAME TIPS

**1** There's no safe space to stand here! You can choose to stay in the middle of the arena, where there's the chance that a hit from a rhino might not be strong enough to knock you out.

LIVING ON THE EDGE ...

**STAT ATTACK**

**2** The problem with that is it's harder to keep track of all three rhinos, and you're more likely to be in their path when they do charge. So you need to be super alert if you stand in the middle.

**3** Standing on the edges means you can angle the camera and watch the rhinos—and you're more likely to have time to leap aside when they charge. But a hit from a rhino here will almost certainly knock you out—you can't rely on the railing to keep you in.

**4** Just before a rhino charges, it'll stop and blow steam—that's the time to jump and dive aside. The rhinos target players, so the fewer players left in the arena, the more likely the rhinos are to target *you*!

YOU GET CHARGED A LOT WHEN YOU COME HERE!

**!**

# TOP TIP
USE THE SPIN OF THE CENTRAL DISC TO INCREASE YOUR SPEED!

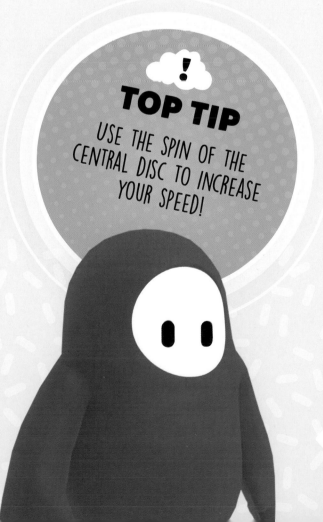

TRY TO KEEP ALL THREE RHINOS IN VIEW.

# BUTTON BASHERS

## WHEN PUSH COMES TO SHOVE, YOU NEED TO HIT MORE BUTTONS THAN YOUR OPPONENT!

This one-on-one round is like Whack-A-Mole—you and another player are dropped into an arena with buttons on the floor that switch force fields, gravity zones, and blizzard fans on and off. One of the buttons lights up yellow—and the first to hit it scores a point!

GO FOR THE MIDDLE BUTTON FIRST!

# GAME TIPS

**1** The center button can only be reached if one of the others is activated by using the force field platform to walk up, or the fans or low gravity to aid your jump. The buttons switch these features on and off whether they're lit up or not.

**2** Using the camera well is really, really important in this round. You need to look around the area quickly and spot which button is lit up. As soon as a button is pushed, whirl that camera around and look for the next one.

**3** In fact, if you can see your opponent is definitely going to reach the next button before you, start looking for the next button *before* it lights up. Get in a position where you can see as much of the arena as possible, and when it lights up you can get a head start!

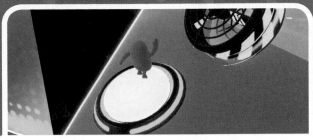

DIVE ON THE BUTTON IF YOU NEED TO!

KEEP AS MANY BUTTONS IN VIEW AS YOU CAN.

**4** You can grab your opponent to slow them down and stop them jumping on buttons. This can be a good tactic if you're ahead in the match—whoever's leading when the time runs out wins, so you can just delay your opponent and run down the clock.

**!**

## TOP TIP

THE CENTER BUTTON IS ALWAYS THE FIRST TO LIGHT UP IN EVERY MATCH.

## 👑 STAT ATTACK

**NUMBER OF PLAYERS:** 2–30 (EVEN NUMBERS ONLY)
**HOW MANY QUALIFY:** 50%
**MAX LENGTH OF ROUND:** 1:30 (5:15 IF MATCH GOES TO OVERTIME)
**INTRODUCED:** SEASON 4.5
**DIFFICULTY RATING:** 3/5

# AIRTIME

## GET YOUR HEAD IN THE ZONE—AND KEEP IT THERE TO WIN THIS GAME!

The purest of all *Fall Guys* rounds? There's no finish line to race toward or tasks to perform, you just have to *not fall*. Jump into the scoring zone and stay on the platforms as long as you can to score points. Falling doesn't eliminate you, so get back in there!

## GAME TIPS

AVOID THIS AREA!

**1** Players spawn next to a Big Swingus, and can grab onto it to drop into the scoring zone. Don't swing across to the central section ahead of you—it's the hardest area to land in, and the hardest to stay on.

**2** Instead, turn the camera while you're on the Big Swingus, let it swing back and then drop down onto the circuit of platforms below—or just use the drum at the side of the spawn point to launch yourself onto them.

##  STAT ATTACK

**NUMBER OF PLAYERS:** 15–45

**HOW MANY QUALIFY:** 60%

**MAX LENGTH OF ROUND:** 5:00

**INTRODUCED:** SEASON 6

**DIFFICULTY RATING:** 3/5

**3** The Drums, Pivot Platform, and Rotating Beam are easiest to stay on. The Pivot Platform flips regularly, but if you jump up and grab one of the Big Swinguses at either end of it, you can hang there until the platform flips back, then drop down.

**4** If you fall, the Slingus Flinguses may seem the quickest way of getting back up, but you can waste a ton of time trying to get them to fling you onto a platform. The vacuum tubes at the bottom, which return you to the spawn point, are a more reliable method.

**!**

**TOP TIP**

YOU SCORE ABOUT 4% FOR EVERY SECOND YOU SPEND IN THE ZONE.

DON'T GET TIPPED BELOW THE SCORING ZONE.

GO FOR THE PIVOT PLATFORM.

# TAIL TAG

## SOMEONE'S ALWAYS ON YOUR TAIL, OR ELSE YOU'RE ON THEIRS!

At the start of this round, half the players have tails and half don't. The players who don't can grab a tail from the ones who do—and if you finish the round with no tail, you'll get eliminated. Either way, you can't afford to stand still!

DON'T STOP MOVING! EVER!!

## GAME TIPS

**1** If you have a tail, remember that all players run at the same speed, which means others chasing behind you will only catch up if you hesitate or don't run in a straight line. So keep up the pace!

**2** Staying close to other players with tails can distract tail-less players from grabbing yours by making it harder to see whether you have a tail or not. Whereas if you're out on your own, you're a more obvious target.

♔ **STAT ATTACK**

**3** If you don't have a tail, don't waste a bunch of time chasing the same player and waiting for them to make a mistake. Change direction and try to run into someone else coming the other way. Predictable movements are the easiest ones to dodge.

**4** There's a team variant of this round, in which all the players are randomly divided into four teams. This is easier to get through than regular Tail Tag, since the three highest scoring teams qualify for the next round.

TARGET THOSE TAILS!

I WONDER IF I STILL HAVE A TAIL ...

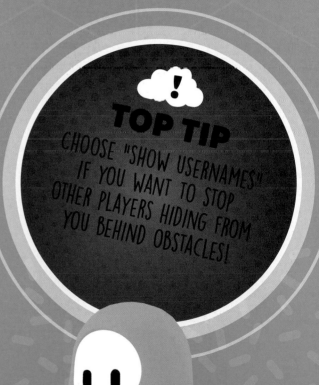

**TOP TIP**

CHOOSE "SHOW USERNAMES" IF YOU WANT TO STOP OTHER PLAYERS HIDING FROM YOU BEHIND OBSTACLES!

△ △ △ △ △ △

# PERFECT MATCH

## A FRUIT-THEMED MEMORY GAME THAT'LL PUT YOUR BRAIN TO THE TEST!

The logic-based rounds are super stressful because they require you to do several things at once. You must memorize things while moving around the arena and making sure other players don't push you off a platform. Stay as calm as you can—none of these tasks are difficult on their own.

REMEMBER ONE OF EACH FRUIT.

A DIFFERENT WAY OF PICKING FRUIT.

# GAME TIPS

**1** In the first stage, tiles will flash with images of fruit. Find a good position to see as much of the grid as possible—and try not to turn around! It's easy to forget which tile is where if you're looking at the grid from different angles.

**2** The rounds get more difficult as it goes on. In the first round, the board will usually be filled with pictures of two different fruits, but the second will usually have four different fruits and the third will have six—meaning there are fewer safe squares.

QUICK! WHERE WERE THE CHERRIES?

**TOP TIP**

DON'T JUST FOLLOW EVERYONE ELSE TO A TILE—THEY MIGHT BE WRONG!

**3** The tiles will go blank and a fruit will appear on the screens. You need to move to a tile that had that fruit on it. So don't try to memorize the whole grid—one tile for each fruit is enough, and ideally they should be next to each other.

**4** In most *Fall Guys* rounds it doesn't help to have a friend in the room, but in this one it does! You can both try to memorize the tiles, or one of you can memorize some of the fruits and the other can look out for the rest.

## ♛ STAT ATTACK

**NUMBER OF PLAYERS:** 30–45
**HOW MANY QUALIFY:** ALL SURVIVORS
**MAX LENGTH OF ROUND:** 1:20
**INTRODUCED:** Beta version
**DIFFICULTY RATING:** 4/5

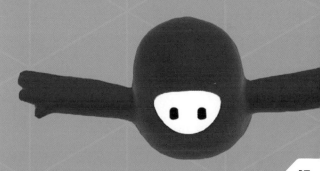

# SUM FRUIT

## THIS MATH-BASED ROUND IS A TRICKY ADDITION TO THE GAME!

As with Perfect Match, your task is to find the safe fruit picture to stand on. However, this offers a different memory challenge—you need to count the giant fruit as it falls, which is then covered by slime, and move to the tile that matches the number on the screens. Got it?

## GAME TIPS

**1** As soon as each round starts, get up on the steps—not only does this give you the best position to reach the tiles, it gives you the best view of the arena. It's easy to miss a fruit if it rolls down the sides.

**2** As with Perfect Match, you may find it useful to have a friend in the room to help! You could even consider having a pen and paper handy—maybe write out the names of the fruits during the loading screens, ready to note the number next to them.

A BERRY GOOD MOVE!

##  STAT ATTACK

**NUMBER OF PLAYERS:** 30–45
**HOW MANY QUALIFY:**
ALL SURVIVORS
**MAX LENGTH OF ROUND:** 1:41
**INTRODUCED:** SEASON 5
**DIFFICULTY RATING:** 4/5

**3** There'll always be a different number of each fruit, so try remembering them in order of quantity—for example, "two bananas, three pears, four coconuts." Jump to the middle tiles while waiting for the number to appear—you'll be able to reach the other tiles quicker.

**4** Compared with Perfect Match, other players are more likely to get this wrong—they may have miscounted, misremembered, or just not spotted one of the fruits. So following everyone to the most popular tile is less likely to work.

**TOP TIP**

IF ZERO APPEARS ON THE SCREENS, MOVE TO A FRUIT THAT DIDN'T FALL AT ALL.

HEAD FOR THE MIDDLE TILES!

TURN THE CAMERA AND GET COUNTING.

# JINXED

## IT'S DEFINITELY NOT ROSY BEING PINK IN THIS GAME!

In this round, all players are split into two teams. At the start, one player from each team is "jinxed" and has a pink haze around them. These players must run around tagging unjinxed players while the rest try to avoid being jinxed. The last unjinxed player wins it for their team!

## GAME TIPS

**1** Getting this round can really mess up a tournament for good *Fall Guys* players, because it all comes down to one player managing to avoid getting jinxed. But if the whole team works hard, you have a chance!

IT'S UP TO YOU—GET 'EM!

### STAT ATTACK

NUMBER OF PLAYERS
(EVEN NUMBERS)
HOW MANY QUALIFY
STARTING THIS ROUND
INTRODUCED
DIFFICULTY RATING: 3/6

**2** If you start off jinxed, it's important to work hard in the first few seconds and give your team a good start, because you'll be the only one doing the jinxing. Once some others get jinxed, your role is less essential.

**3** The more players on a team to get jinxed, the more players that team has to hunt down unjinxed opposition players. So the game is harder for whichever team is in the lead. This means a round of Jinxed is usually very close!

**4** If you avoid getting jinxed, you can try running with others of your team who have been jinxed—opponents may not notice you don't have a pink cloud around you. But this can be risky, since your teammates won't be staying away from the other team!

JUST MY LUCK TO GET THIS ROUND ...

**! TOP TIP**

DON'T FOCUS TOO HARD ON ONE AREA—YOU DON'T WANT TO LOSE THIS BECAUSE ONE BEAN HID IN A CORNER!

FIND SOMEONE TO JINX—QUICK!

# PEGWIN PURSUIT

## GRAB ONE OF THOSE SLIPPERY SEABIRDS AND HOLD ONTO IT FOR YOUR TEAM!

In this round all players are split into three teams, with four to seven players on each team. There are also three pegwins, which you must try to grab. You score a point for every second you keep hold of a pegwin. The two teams with the highest score qualify!

THEY'RE AFTER YOUR PEGWIN! RUN AWAY!!

## GAME TIPS

**1** The obvious way to play this round is for everyone to focus on chasing down the pegwins: either trying to grab the ones who are free, or trying to grab your opponents to make them drop theirs.

**2** However, if one or more of your teammates already has a pegwin, you may prefer to focus on frustrating the other teams' attempts to take it, by grabbing them. Don't spend too long holding back one player—keep following your teammate and protecting them.

DON'T GET GRABBED!

**3** Don't forget, you don't need to win, just not finish last. So focus on taking pegwins from the team in last place. If you're in last place, focus on the team in second, because you need to overtake them, not the winners.

**4** Be aware that, if the bottom two teams are tied when the timer runs out, 15 seconds of overtime will be played, and then another 15 seconds, until one team edges ahead.

**!**

## TOP TIP

TURNSTILES, HAMMERS, AND ANYTHING THAT KNOCKS YOU OVER WILL MAKE YOU DROP YOUR PEGWIN.

## ♛ STAT ATTACK

**NUMBER OF PLAYERS:** 12–21 (ONLY MULTIPLES OF 3)
**HOW MANY QUALIFY:** 67%
**MAX LENGTH OF ROUND:** 2:00
**INTRODUCED:** SEASON 3
**DIFFICULTY RATING:** 4/5

# ROCK 'N' ROLL

## YOUR "ROLL" IN THIS ROUND IS TO GET THE BALL OVER THE FINISH LINE!

In this round you're split into three teams and must roll a giant ball through an obstacle course, down a slope, and into a goal. The first two teams to get their ball over the line qualify. Initially you're all stuck in your lanes, but in the final stretch you're all together!

## GAME TIPS

**1** The important part of this round is that final lane, because at that point you can cross over and interfere with the other teams' progress. If you can get there ahead of the other teams, you'll have a big advantage.

**2** Some of you need to push the ball from behind, others need to go for the sides to direct it. Don't grab for the ball—it doesn't help and you'll probably end up grabbing one of your teammates, holding them back.

YOU'RE BETTER OFF IN THE MIDDLE.

## ♛ STAT ATTACK

**NUMBER OF PLAYERS:** 15–30 (MULTIPLES OF 3 ONLY)
**HOW MANY QUALIFY:** 67%
**MAX LENGTH OF ROUND:** 3:00
**INTRODUCED:** Beta version
**DIFFICULTY RATING:** 3/5

**3** You'll often see one or two teammates run on ahead. This isn't because they can't be bothered to help roll the ball—they're going to hold up the other teams if they get to the final lane first. If you don't see anyone else doing this—go for it.

**4** When sabotaging other teams, remember only one team will be eliminated, so focus on holding up the team that's furthest behind. It's also easier to hold up a team that's come from a side lane—you can push their ball against the wall.

TOP TIP

WATCH OUT FOR THE VARIANT WITH MOVING DONUT BUMPERS!

PUSH, DON'T GRAB!

KEEP THE BALL ON COURSE—STRAIGHT AS YOU CAN.

# FALL BALL

## THE GOAL IS OBVIOUS IN THIS SOCCER-STYLE ROUND!

The *Fall Guys* version of soccer is a bit like *Rocket League* without the cars—there's a giant ball and giant goals. However, there's also another ball, which complicates things. There are variants of this game where the soccer ball is replaced by a football, a banana, or a golden egg worth five points!

KEEP YOUR EYE ON BOTH BALLS!

## GAME TIPS

**1** Real-life team sports rely on communication and all the members of the team understanding their roles. There's no chance for that in *Fall Guys*, but you still need to make sure some of you defend while some of you attack!

## STAT ATTACK

NUMBER OF PLAYERS: 8-20 (EVEN NUMBERS ONLY)
HOW MANY QUALIFY: 50%
MAX LENGTH OF ROUND: 2:00
INTRODUCED: Beta version
DIFFICULTY RATING: 3/5

**2** This game changes depending on how many players are involved. If it's ten-a-side, you can afford one player to just hang back and defend your goal. If it's four-a-side, all four of you will need to work on getting control of the balls.

**3** After a goal is scored, the ball will respawn in the middle of the field – a shadow will show where it's going to land. Try to hit it toward your opponent's goal as it falls—you can use its momentum to send it further than usual.

**4** Getting the ball to go in the right direction can be hard, so work together—a group of you has a better chance of getting the ball moving. A bouncing ball is more difficult to control, but also more difficult to defend.

SOME VARIANTS HAVE OBSTACLES.

GLAD WE DON'T HAVE TO USE OUR TINY FEET...

**TOP TIP**

IF A PEGWIN APPEARS, IGNORE IT—YOU CAN'T USE IT TO SCORE POINTS.

# LOST TEMPLE

## NAVIGATE THIS LABYRINTH OF FAKE DOORS TO CLAIM VICTORY!

This Final round drives a lot of players crazy! You must make your way through a series of rooms containing obstacles you'll have encountered in other rounds, and a mix of real and fake doors. The rooms are random and so are the fake doors, so you can't learn the path!

## GAME TIPS

**1** If you've played Gate Crash, you'll know it's important to watch other players! If you see them run into a fake door, go for one of the others. If you fall behind in this round, don't worry—you'll probably get a chance to catch up.

ANYONE TRIED THAT DOOR ...?

**2** Rooms in the middle of the map have a higher chance of the real door being to the left or right, because the game is programmed to stop players getting forward too quickly. At the edges of the map, try the front door first.

**3** The route never takes you to a dead end and never creates a closed loop, so try to remember where you've already been, because if you can see that a door leads to a room you've passed through, it'll be fake.

**4** The last two rooms aren't random—one is a series of conveyor belts, leading to a real door which takes you to the final room. This contains the crown, which is above a pair of lily pads and moves from side to side.

WHO KNOWS WHAT'S REAL AND WHAT'S FAKE?!

**! TOP TIP**

JUMP INTO THE DOORS, DON'T WALK THROUGH THEM—THERE'S A SMALL STEP AT THE BASE OF EACH ONE.

IF IT'S FAKE, TURN QUICK!

# FALL MOUNTAIN

## KEEP YOUR EYES ON THE PRIZE ... AND ON THE BALLS TRYING TO KNOCK YOU DOWN!

This classic Final round works exactly like a Race round except only one can win it. By this stage, only top players will still be in, so you can't afford to make any mistakes!

SO NEAR—AND YET SO FAR!

# GAME TIPS

**1** Definitely watch the opening cutscene to check out what's ahead—there are several possible variants of this round. For instance, sometimes there are conveyor belts at the sides—if they're there and you spawn at one side, use them!

DON'T JUST STAND THERE—MOVE!

**2** The hardest part of this round is dealing with the balls—they're random and you can't plan for them! Angle your camera upward to help you see them coming. When you get further up, use the diamond blocks as cover.

DON'T FLIP OUT NOW ...

**3** There are hammers on the final paths to the top—if taking the right path, go to the left of the hammer. If taking the left path, go to the right side. The timing is still tricky but going in the same direction as the hammer helps!

**4** You need to *grab* the crown when you reach it—don't just try to touch it and *definitely* don't try to dive. You'll probably have to be quick, because other players will be right behind you—but pay attention to the height of the crown and time your grab!

**!**

## TOP TIP

IF THERE'S A LOW GRAVITY ZONE, AVOID JUMPING INSIDE IT.

## ♛ STAT ATTACK

**NUMBER OF PLAYERS:** 2-9
**HOW MANY QUALIFY:** 1
**MAX LENGTH OF ROUND:** 5:00
**INTRODUCED:** Beta version
**DIFFICULTY RATING:** 5/5

# HEX-A-GONE

## HOP BETWEEN THE HEXAGONS TO GET YOUR HANDS ON THE PRIZE!

In this round, players start on a grid of hexagons. The moment a hexagon is touched, it starts to flash and then disappears. If you fall through the hole, you'll land on another grid of hexagons. After falling through several layers, you'll end up in the slime—the last one standing wins!

## GAME TIPS

THAT TILE'S GONNA BE GONE!

**1** New players are advised to stay away from others on this round—stake out your own turf and work on it. Angle your camera so you can see the layer below and find somewhere to land when you eventually do fall.

**2** You can cross a one-hexagon gap with a normal jump, and you can cross a two-hexagon gap with a jump and dive. Jumping means you spend less time in contact with the hexagons, so it will usually help you survive longer than running.

##  STAT ATTACK

**NUMBER OF PLAYERS:** 4–12
**HOW MANY QUALIFY:** 1
**MAX LENGTH OF ROUND:** 5:00
**INTRODUCED:** Beta version
**DIFFICULTY RATING:** 5/5

**3** Experienced players can try some sneaky strategy—running or grabbing to knock others down to the next level, or deliberately going down a level to eat up tiles underneath other players. If you're especially bold, you can drop down to the bottom level and methodically destroy it!

**4** Very rarely, this can appear as early as Round 1, with 40 or more players competing for space! If this does happen, players around you may eat up the tiles quickly, leaving little time for strategy. Just jump and hope for the best!

! TOP TIP

IF THERE ARE VACANT SPAWN TILES NEAR YOU, JUMP TO THOSE FIRST.

LEAVE NOWHERE FOR OTHERS TO LAND.

DON'T GET IN EACH OTHER'S WAY—YOU'LL PROBABLY BOTH FALL!

# MY FALL GUYS FAVES AND HATES!

**My favorite round is** .............................

**My favorite theme is** .............................

**My trickiest round is** .............................

**My most hated obstacle is** ...................

**My favorite outfit is** ...........................

**My favorite pattern is** .........................

**My favorite color scheme is** ................